Happy Thanksgiving Birthday

by

Samantha Bresnehan and Adrienne Drost

Illustrated by Lisa Powell Braun

Happy Thanksgiving Birthday

by
Samantha Bresnehan and Adrienne Drost

This book belongs to

_____

who was born on Thanksgiving,

November _____

Happy Thanksgiving Birthday

Text © 2023 by Samantha Bresnehan and Adrienne Drost

Illustrations © 2023 by Lisa Powell Braun at lisa-powell-braun.com

Published by Big & Baby Books LLC

All Rights Reserved.

No part of this book may be used or reproduced in any manner whatsoever without written permission from the author except in the case of brief quotations embodied in critical articles or reviews.

ISBN: 979-8-9885711-2-4

S.B. - *For my nieces, Lilly and Meredith, who both have Thanksgiving week birthdays.*

A.D. - *For my granddaughter, Meredith, who was born on Thanksgiving eve.*

L.B. - *For Marc, Ian and Deirdre*

Thanksgiving Day is celebrated in the United States each year on the fourth Thursday of November.

So, if your birthday is at the end of November, in some years your birthday and Thanksgiving will be on the same day! Happy Thanksgiving Birthday! Have you ever met someone else who shares the same birthday as you?

Thanksgiving is a national holiday which celebrates the historical meal shared by the Pilgrims and the Indigenous peoples.

Together they gave thanks for peace and a bountiful harvest. This is one of the oldest traditions in America.

Today we celebrate Thanksgiving by gathering with our families and friends who often spend the day or sometimes the whole weekend together at someone's home.

Thanksgiving travel is the busiest time on the roads and in the skies! Where will you spend Thanksgiving?

As you might have guessed by its name, this holiday is all about giving THANKS! Can you think of something you are thankful for on your Thanksgiving birthday?

Delicious meal!

The Thanksgiving season is also a wonderful time to give back to others and share food, clothes or other items.

Getting involved with a Thanksgiving collection is a nice way to give back to your community. Since you will be getting lots of new presents for your birthday, will you donate to someone in need?

A Thanksgiving birthday guarantees you won't be in school on your birthday. No tests, projects or homework. Schools are closed on Thanksgiving Day and usually the next day too. It's a four-day weekend for your birthday!

November

S	M	T	W	TH	F	S

HAPPY BIRTHDAY!

Planning your Thanksgiving birthday party might take a little more thought since late November is a busy time of year. It will be fun to celebrate with your family and other guests on Thanksgiving Day.

But, it's probably a good idea to plan a party with friends the week before or even after Thanksgiving when everyone is home.

Thanksgiving preparations begin with planning the meal and inviting family and friends over.

A "Friendsgiving" birthday party is one way to celebrate with your friends. Sharing and making food together is a nice way to build your friendships.

Thanksgiving morning often starts with a hometown parade. The famous Macy's Thanksgiving Day parade in New York City has giant balloons, floats, marching bands and even a visit from Santa at the very end. Now the countdown to Christmas begins! Will you watch a parade this year?

Thanksgiving Day football is an American tradition that first began in the late 1800's. Today, football games are played across the country from hometown fields to college and professional stadiums.

Will you watch a game on TV or go see one in person? You might even play football with your guests in the backyard or a local park.
Touchdown— Thanksgiving birthday!

Sharing a big meal is one of the highlights of Thanksgiving Day. Traditional foods like turkey, potatoes, corn, cranberry sauce and pumpkin pie are almost always served as a reminder of the first Thanksgiving feast. Guests often bring a special dish to share with everyone. What is your favorite Thanksgiving food?

You might "stuff" yourself with all the delicious holiday food but be sure to save room for dessert. Besides pumpkin and apple pies, it's time for birthday cake!

Happy Thanksgiving,
Happy Birthday,
and
Happy Thanksgiving Birthday!

Happy Thanksgiving Birthday

Your birthday holds a very special place on the calendar and is the start of your new year. Holidays are also important dates on the calendar. Celebrating them together can be busy but double the fun! Since fewer babies are born on holidays, having a holiday birthday makes you even more unique.

The way you celebrate your birthday may change each year, but having a holiday birthday is forever special.

Top 10 Least Common Birthdays*

RANK	DATE	U.S. AVERAGE NUMBER OF BABIES BORN
1	December 25	6,574
2	January 1	7,792
3	December 24	8,069
4	July 4	8,796
5	January 2	9,307
6	December 26	9,543
7	November 27	9,718
8	November 23	9,883
9	November 25	9,954
10	October 31	9,978

*Data: U.S. National Center for Health Statistics (1994-2003) and U.S. Social Security Administration (2004-2014)

Here's a space for you to write about your day, draw pictures, include photos or have your friends and family write a birthday note to you.

Big & Baby Books
Read together.

Big & Baby Books aims to inspire parents, siblings, and others to begin reading to children early and often. We support the well-documented benefits of reading, including developing language and analytical skills, creativity, and improved focus and concentration.

Reading *together* does that and more- it strengthens bonding and helps children express their feelings and ideas.

Our books are meaningful, durable, and playful. They will hold a special place on your child's bookshelf.

About the Authors

Samantha Bresnehan lives in Rio Rancho, New Mexico with her husband, two children, and two dogs. Reading with her children is one of her favorite things so it was only natural to begin writing books for them and other kids, too!

Adrienne Drost is married and the mother of two adult children. She lives in Las Vegas, Nevada where she enjoys both the city and nature. An avid reader and occasional writer, it was becoming "Grammie" that inspired her to write children's literature in collaboration with her daughter, Samantha.

Please visit *BigandBabyBooks.com* to learn more about our story and other titles in the holiday birthday series.

www.ingramcontent.com/pod-product-compliance
Lightning Source LLC
Chambersburg PA
CBHW061406010526
44119CB00011B/270